fast fun & easy

FABRIC FLOWERS

beautiful blooms in an afternoon

Karen Flamme

C&T PUBLISHING

Text © 2005 Karen Flamme

Artwork © 2005 C&T Publishing, Inc.

Publisher: Amy Marson

Editorial Director: Gailen Runge

Acquisitions Editor: Jan Grigsby

Editor: Stacy Chamness

Technical Editor: Ellen Pahl

Copyeditor: Wordfirm Inc.

Cover Designer: Kristen Yenche

Design Director: Kristy Zacharias

Production Artist: Kirstie L. Pettersen

Production Assistant: Kerry Graham

Illustrator: Kiera Lofgreen

Photography: C&T Publishing, Inc.

Published by C&T Publishing, Inc.,
P.O. Box 1456, Lafayette, CA 94549

Library of Congress Cataloging-in-Publication Data

Flamme, Karen

Fast, fun & easy fabric flowers : beautiful blooms in an afternoon / Karen Flamme.

    p. cm.

ISBN 1-57120-318-4 (paper trade)

1. Fabric flowers.

TT890.5F53 2005

746–dc22

2005017587

Printed in China   10 9 8 7 6 5 4 3 2 1

Acknowledgments

Producing a book takes a lot of people: some inspire, support, and encourage, and others edit, design, market, or distribute. I'm very lucky to have had lots of help from wonderful people in all these areas, and many more.

Inspiration came early in my life from three special women. My grandmother's hands were never idle. Her quilts hang on our walls, and we use her embroidered and needlepoint pieces daily. My mother loved digging in the garden and waiting for spring flowers to bloom, particularly petunias in every imaginable color. My special Auntie showered me with books and fanned every creative spark to make me believe that with curiosity and imagination, anything is possible.

Thank goodness for my wonderful family, friends, quilting buddies, and students. Extra-special thanks go to:

• My quilting mini-group pals, Claudia Comay, Carolyn Hill, Diane Kern, Jean Lehman, Chris Renner, and Marcia Stein, who inspire and motivate me

• Marilyn Cox (Lee too!) for years of friendship, fun, and support; and the rest of the morning coffee crowd, both two- and four-legged, for their warmth and good humor

• Gail Abeloe and her fantastic staff at Back Porch Fabrics in Pacific Grove, California, where enthusiasm and creativity are contagious

This book would still be in my computer without the great C&T family members listed on the left, plus fabulous photographers Diane Pedersen and Luke Mulks

Most importantly, my life wouldn't be fun at all without my wonderful family. My husband, John, still tries to count all the pieces in quilts and loves being in the minority at quilt shows. My daughter, Jennifer, is a never-ending source of good ideas, encouragement, and delight. I couldn't wish for better companions on my creative journey.

Contents

Introduction

Throw away your watering can and forget about green thumbs! If you can use scissors and an iron you can have a roomful of fabric flowers in no time. The flowers in this book are fun and easy to make. The rules are few and flexible, and the projects are perfect for all ages. In fact, there are some special tips for children scattered throughout the pages. You can even make many of the flowers without any sewing at all.

Gardening and playing with fabric are two of my favorite hobbies. I guess it's not surprising that I would find a way to combine them. It was winter, nothing much was blooming, and I wanted flowers for a party. That's where it all began!

Fabric flowers are just plain fun to make. You don't need to know how to sew, or cut precisely, or match points; you just need to follow a few directions and not be afraid to experiment. This book is really all about playing with fabric—finding color combinations you like, looking for unusual textures, and experimenting with fabric paints, glitter, and embellishments. You can make the flowers as simple, or as fancy, as your time and spirit allow.

I'll get you started with basic flower shapes and styles, and show you some ideas for embellishing and individualizing, then you're on your own to sow seeds of creativity and reap the rewards.

Time to get busy and grow your garden. Read All the Basics, beginning on the next page, then pick a flower you want to start with and dig right in.

all the basics

Flower making, like gardening, is easiest if you have all your tools close at hand. Use this guide to help you gather equipment, select fabrics, and learn unfamiliar terms and techniques. You'll notice that the basics are quite similar for all the flowers. They begin with a basic fabric sandwich: fabric on top and bottom, with a stiffening agent (stabilizer) in the middle. When you browse the Ideas & Inspiration pages (58–59) you'll see some ways to use fabric flowers. I'm sure you will be able to think of many, many more!

Selecting fabrics is lots of fun because almost anything works! Prints, florals, plaids, batiks, and solids are just a few of the fabrics you'll want to try. I'll show you how different the same flower can look when you change the fabric and finishing touches. Then you'll have fun experimenting on your own.

Basic Materials

fabrics

I suggest using cotton fabric for your first flower, just to get the feel of the process, but any fabric that can be ironed and fused works very well. Pull out your favorite scraps, too, because most flowers take less than a 10″ square.

A big part of the fun of making flowers is experimenting with different fabrics. Keep in mind the mood you want to create and how you will use the flowers as you select fabric: polka dots and small prints are playful and whimsical, solids can be dramatic, and batiks and geometrics are softer and more sophisticated. Sheer and silky fabrics guarantee a dainty or elegant look. Of course, embellishments and stitching make each eye-catching bloom unique. Let your imagination go and add your own touches. No two flowers in your fabric garden will be exactly alike—just as in nature!

fun!

Look for sparkly, shiny, and textured novelty fabrics. Test them first to be sure they won't melt when ironed!

stabilizers

Stabilizers, or stiffening agents, provide the middle layer in the fabric sandwich in many of the flowers. Stabilizers are purchased by the yard and are available at your local fabric store, online, or by mail order. See Sources on page 63.

I've had good luck with several products; for each flower I suggest which one I think works best.

Fast2fuse Double-Sided Fusible Stiff Interfacing is an interfacing with fusible adhesive on both sides. This has a definite advantage in terms of both time and ease of handling over interfacings that aren't fusible. Fast2fuse is best suited to cottons and stiffer flowers.

easy!

Fuse cotton fabrics to both sides of the fast2fuse and toss the fabric sandwich in the washer and dryer before cutting out the flower. This gives it a softer, wrinkled, heirloom look.

Timtex is a little softer than fast2fuse and does not have a fusible coating, so you'll need to add a fusible web layer to both sides. It is another good option for cottons and flowers with satin-stitched edges.

Canvas, denim, and duck fabrics, all 100% cotton, can also be used as stabilizers for softer, floppier flowers. Because these fabrics are thinner than fast2fuse or Timtex, they're perfect for no-sew flowers. I always use white or natural so the center layer doesn't show through the outer fabric. For these stabilizers, you need to add fusible web to both sides.

easy!

Another benefit of fusing is that fused fabrics don't fray when you cut them.

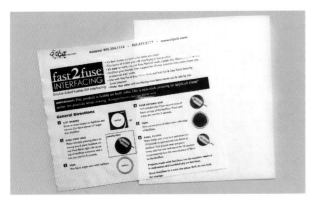

Fusibles come with application directions.

fusible web

Fusible web is used to bond two layers of fabric together. There are many kinds on the market, and you may want to try several before you settle on one you like best. My favorite is Pellon Wonder Under. It comes in several weights and is a good stabilizer for delicate or sheer fabrics. For best results, always follow the manufacturer's instructions that come with the fusible.

fun!

Add color and interest to flowers by using different fabrics on the front and the back.

easy!

Life is easier and your iron and ironing board are much cleaner if you make sure the paper backing of the fusible web is facing the iron and the glue side is touching the *wrong* side of the fabric (not the iron!) before you begin to iron.

thread

Most of the basic flowers don't require any sewing, but I'm sure that you will find yourself experimenting with satin stitching the edges, adding embellishments, outlining veins on leaves, and on and on! It's your choice whether to use a thread color that blends with the fabric or something that contrasts. I like solid or variegated cotton or rayon thread, but it's fun to use sparkly thread too. Whatever you choose, your sewing machine will probably like it better if you use the same thread in the bobbin as on the top.

fast!

Use leftover fabric-sandwich scraps to test a few stitches before you begin sewing on the real flower. Adjust the stitch length and width and tension if needed.

easy!

If your sewing machine has a needle-down option, use it for satin stitching. Your stitches won't slip as you pivot and turn or stop and start.

buttons

Here's your chance to use those buttons you've been saving, or to look for some of the fun novelty buttons on the market. (Who wouldn't want to spot a ladybug button in the center of a daisy?) Buttons are the center that holds the stem in many of the flowers. It's best if the buttons have fairly large holes or shanks so the stem wire can slip through easily.

fun!

Select a big button for the center, then find a smaller contrasting one to put on top of it. Layer the buttons and insert the stem wire through both.

floral stem wire

Flower stems are made from purchased floral stem wire and fastened with floral stem tape. You can buy these in packages wherever craft or floral supplies are sold. Floral stem wire is sold by gauge (thickness); the bigger the number, the thinner the wire. You'll probably be able to choose between plain, cloth-wrapped, and paper-wrapped wire. I prefer paper-wrapped 18-gauge wire for the sturdy, thick stems of upright flowers. For more pliable stems, use a higher number than 18-gauge.

Thin, unwrapped floral stem wire (about 24-gauge) is thin enough to fuse in the center of the fabric sandwich. This can help give shape to sheer petals and make leaves bendable.

fast!

Having trouble finding prewrapped wire? Go to the hardware store, buy bulk wire the thickness you want, and wrap it yourself with floral stem tape.

floral stem tape

Green ½˝-wide floral stem tape, or stem wrap, comes in rolls and fastens the flower and leaves to the stem. It also gives the stem a finishing wrap. Stretch it as you wrap and it sticks to itself; it's easy to use.

Basic Supplies

If you sew or do craft projects, you probably have most of these items already. They are basic cutting, sewing, marking, and ironing tools. I've suggested specific equipment and sizes that work for me, but you may be able to adapt what you already have, even if it isn't exactly what I suggest. You won't need any special gardening tools for these flowers!

cutting

You need at least two pairs of sharp scissors: one for cutting paper and template materials, and the other for cutting fabric. One pair should have pointed blades that can poke a hole through fabric.

I use a medium-sized rotary cutter (45mm) and mat for most of my cutting. It's an easy way to cut through multiple layers of fabric and fast2fuse or Timtex. A small rotary cutter (28mm) is helpful when cutting curves on some of the flower and leaf shapes as well. An 18″ × 24″ rotary-cutting mat is a good size for these projects. Be very careful when using the rotary cutter around the flower shapes; you can use scissors if you prefer.

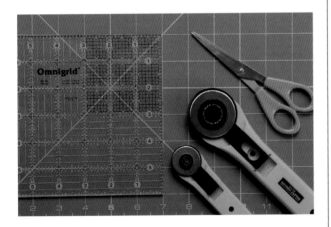

easy!

If you're having trouble cutting through multiple layers with a rotary cutter, replace the blade with a new one. A new blade makes smoother cuts and is easier on your hand.

You'll also need a see-through rotary ruler, at least 6″ × 12″, to measure and cut through interfacing, fabric, and fusible web.

A pair of wire snips or pliers with a wire cutter are useful for cutting and bending stems.

ironing

Your iron needs both a steam and a dry setting. Most fusibles require a dry iron, and you'll want to steam the wrinkles out of your flower fabric before you begin. A regular ironing board is fine, but be sure to put a pressing sheet over it to protect the cover when you are ironing fusibles.

No matter how careful I am, it seems that sticky spots of fusible always appear on my iron when I am through with one of these projects. A quick fix is to keep a tube of hot iron cleaner on hand. You can find it at most hardware or grocery stores. Just rub it onto the hot iron faceplate with an old towel and the fusible glue remnants disappear.

easy!

Check your iron for dirty spots each time you finish the fusing step. It's much easier than trying to get black blobs off a pink petal!

marking

A wipe-off chalk marker or erasable fabric-marking pencil is useful for tracing patterns and marking flower centers.

making templates

Patterns are included for some of the flowers. You can make templates by tracing the patterns onto tracing paper, freezer paper, or template plastic.

sewing machine

The basic flowers do not require sewing, so I've put sewing machine at the end of the basic supplies list. Many flower makers use their machines to experiment and add their own touches by satin stitching the edges of flowers or leaves and adding decorative stitching or embellishments, but it certainly isn't essential. Children (and adults!) who have not yet mastered the use of a sewing machine can still have lots of fun making beautiful flowers.

Jen's Closet, Karen Flamme, 33¼″ x 29¼″. Embellish your wardrobe and your quilts with dimensional flowers.

daisy—single and double

Any time of year is perfect for growing fabric daisies. Here are two varieties—single and double—to get your garden started. Make one of these simple daisies to learn the basic techniques, then branch out and try other flowers.

What You'll Need

Basic Supplies:

See All the Basics, pages 5–10.

Fabric:

Start with cotton until you get the feel of making flowers.

Single Daisy:

☐ 2 squares, at least 8″ × 8″, of complementary fabrics

Double Daisy:

☐ 2 squares, at least 8″ × 8″, of 2 fabrics for outer petals

☐ 2 squares, at least 5″ × 5″, of 2 other fabrics for flower center

Fusible:

Regular or heavyweight fusible web such as Pellon Wonder Under

☐ 1 square, at least 8″ × 8″, for single daisy

☐ 1 rectangle, at least 8″ × 13″, for double daisy

Note: This flower does not need a heavy stabilizer layer. It's easier to attach the flower to the stem if the fabric is fairly soft and pliable.

easy!

These measurements make a rather large flower. If you want yours smaller, just start with smaller fabric squares.

fun!

Make daisies in various sizes for a more interesting bouquet.

Notions:

☐ 1 button with at least 2 holes (or a shank) for the flower center that matches or contrasts with the fabrics—you choose!

☐ Wrapped 18-gauge floral stem wire (The length depends on how long you want the stem to be. I usually use an 18″ piece as it comes from the package and trim it later if I don't want it that long.)

☐ Roll of green floral stem tape

fast!

To sew or not to sew? It's your choice. This is a perfect starter flower for kids because no sewing is required. Of course, you can always satin stitch the edges and machine embellish if you want.

How-Tos

cutting

Use a rotary cutter, mat, and ruler to cut the following:

Single Daisy:

☐ 2 squares, 8″ × 8″, one each of 2 complementary fabrics

☐ 1 square, 8″ × 8″, of fusible web

Double Daisy:

☐ 2 squares, 8″ × 8″, one each of 2 complementary fabrics for outer flower

☐ 1 square, 8″ × 8″, of fusible web

☐ 2 squares, 5″ × 5″, one each of 2 complementary fabrics for flower center

☐ 1 square, 5″ × 5″, of fusible web

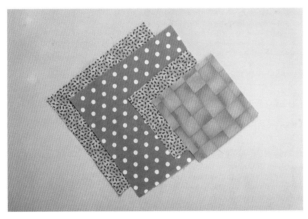

2 sets of fabric squares

fusing

Single and Double Daisy:

1. Iron (on a dry setting) the 8″ square of fusible web to the wrong side of one 8″ fabric square.

2. Peel the paper backing off.

3. Carefully place the wrong side of the second 8″ square of fabric on the fused side of the first square and iron, fusing the two squares together.

Fuse squares with right sides out.

Double Daisy only:

Repeat Steps 1 through 3 using the 5″ squares of fabric and fusible web.

fast!

Put a pressing cloth on your ironing board before you begin fusing to keep it clean.

easy!

For young children, use brightly colored felt squares and cut out flower shapes with blunt-end scissors. No fusing is required for these floppy, fun flowers!

cutting flower shapes

Single and Double Daisy:

1. Use a compass, or a round shape you can trace around (plate, cup, lid), to make a circle about 6″ in diameter in the center of the 8″ fabric sandwich. Be sure your chalk or pencil marker will rub off.

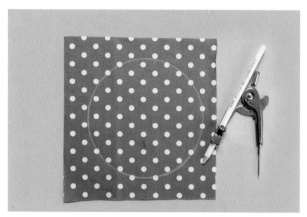

2. Using the circle as a guide for the outer flower shape, you will create petals as you cut. Use scissors to cut out the flower shape, adding free-form scallops outside the chalk circle guideline. The flower is more interesting if the scallops aren't perfect, so don't worry if they are a little uneven. I cut 10 or so petals on the samples, but you can cut the number that looks good to you.

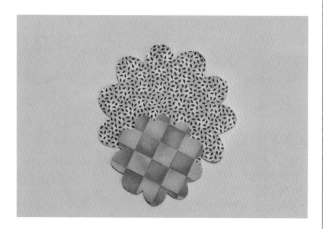

Double Daisy only:

Repeat Steps 1 and 2 above using the 5″ fabric sandwich square. Trace a 3″-diameter circle as a cutting guide for the petals.

fun!

Want to fancy up your flower with stitching, painting, or embellishing? Do it while the petal circles are flat, before you begin assembling them.

assembling

Single and Double Daisy:

1. Insert floral stem wire up through the underside of the button and out one hole.

2. Bend the top 1½″ of wire completely over and insert it back down through the second hole to the underside of the button.

Insert wire up through underside of button and back down through other hole.

3. Twist the short end of the wire around the long end to secure the button on the wire.

4. Poke a small hole in the center of each fused circle using the pointed end of a scissor blade.

Single Daisy:

5. Insert the stem wire through the hole in the center of the fabric flower. Pull the flower up to the button center.

Insert stem through center of daisy.

easy!

Double Daisy:

5. Insert the stem wire through the hole in the small fabric circle and then the large fabric circle. Pull the circles up to the button flower center.

Layer small circle on top of large and insert stem wire.

Single and Double Daisy:

6. Hold the outer edges of the large circle together over the top of the button.

easy!

Wire pieces of glitter sticks to a button for a festive, sparkly touch.

fun!

Sew around the edge of a large petal section using decorative machine stitches and a contrasting color or fancy thread.

7. Use your other hand to pull the center of the circle together on the underside and gather about ½″ of fabric tightly around the wire stem.

8. Hold the gathered fabric and wrap floral stem tape tightly around it.

Gather fabric on stem and wrap tightly with floral tape.

9. Continue wrapping until the fabric is held securely to the wire stem.

Optional: If you want to add leaves, make them following the directions on pages 53–57.

10. Wrap tape down the length of the stem to cover it. Hold the stem in one hand and twist it while stretching and winding the tape with the other.

Your everlasting, no-wilt daisies are now ready to be arranged and displayed!

fun!

Make a wearable daisy pin by following all the instructions above, except substitute shorter, thinner (20-gauge) wire. Cut the stem to about 2″ and wrap it around a purchased pin base.

Variations

A and B: Wrap eyelash yarn around wire on top of the button for a fluffy daisy center.

C: In place of a button, string beads onto a wire, bend it into a circle, and twist it around the stem.

D: Use decorative machine stitches to embellish outer petals before assembling the flower.

E: If you select a shank button for the center, thread the stem wire underneath the button.

F: Single layers of felt make colorful, quick daisies.

G: Add even more petal layers to your daisies.

sunflower

I love sunflowers! Bright, happy, and showy, they are impossible to ignore. Fabric sunflowers attract a lot of attention too. Make them big or small, funky or country, sew or no-sew. They couldn't be easier to make and the variations are endless.

What You'll Need

Basic Supplies:

See All the Basics, pages 5–10.

Fabric:

☐ 1 rectangle, at least 5″ × 10″, of fabric for flower center

☐ 1 rectangle, at least 7″ × 14″, of contrasting fabric for outer petals

Fusible:

☐ 1 square, 5″ × 5″, of fast2fuse

☐ 1 square, 7″ × 7″, of fusible web such as Wonder Under

Notions:

☐ 1 button with at least 2 holes (or shank) for flower center

☐ Wrapped 18-gauge floral stem wire

☐ Roll of green floral stem tape

easy!

Use fabric scraps for a "pieced" flower center. Lay out the cut pieces on a center circle of fast2fuse (4″ in diameter). Fuse them directly to the fast2fuse and trim the edges even with the circle. No sewing needed!

fun!

Start with a bigger petal circle and make big, spiky petals.

How-Tos

cutting

Use a rotary cutter, mat, and ruler to cut the following:

☐ 2 squares, 5″ × 5″, from flower center fabric

☐ 2 squares, 7″ × 7″ from petal fabric

fusing

Flower Center:

Place a 5″ square of center fabric right side up on a 5″ square of fast2fuse and press with a hot, dry iron for 5 seconds. Do not fuse the second 5″ square to the other side yet.

Flower Petals:

Iron a 7″ square of fusible web to the wrong side of a 7″ square of petal fabric. Peel the paper backing off the fusible. Carefully place the wrong side of the second 7″ square of petal fabric on the fused side of the first square and iron, fusing the 2 fabric squares together, right sides out.

easy!

Protect your ironing board by putting a nonstick pressing sheet or parchment baking paper under the fast2fuse when ironing.

cutting flower centers

1. Cut a 4″-diameter circle out of the 5″ square of fabric fused to the fast2fuse.

2. Cut a matching 4″-diameter circle out of the *unfused* 5″ square of flower center fabric.

Cut 2 circles 4″ in diameter.

fast!

Layer the fused square and the unfused square and cut through both layers at once.

fun!

Add a third flower center. Cut a 3″-diameter circle of contrasting fabric with fusible web on the wrong side. Fuse it on top of the 4″ fabric circle to make an inner center.

cutting flower petals

1. Cut a 6″-diameter circle out of the fused 7″ square of petal fabric. Mark the center of the circle.

2. Use scissors to free-form cut petal spikes all around the circle. Make the cuts no deeper than 1″.

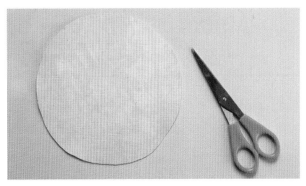

Cut circle from fused petal fabric.

Cut petal spikes with scissors.

3. Using the center mark as a guide, draw a 3″-diameter circle in the middle of the petal unit. Cut out the circle and discard (or see the *easy!* tip below).

Cut center circle out of petal unit.

easy!

Save the circle cutout and fuse it to a larger flower center later as a decorative inner center.

assembling

1. Place the petal unit on a protective pressing cloth on the ironing board.

2. Place the flower center fusible side down (fabric side up) on top of the petal unit.

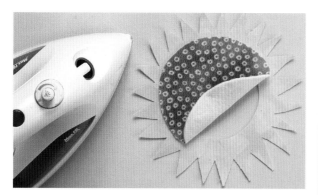

Flower center on top of petals ready to be ironed

3. Use a hot, dry iron to fuse the center to the petals.

4. Turn the piece over and position the remaining 4″ center circle on the back of the petals, with the wrong side of the fabric facing the fast2fuse. Fuse the circle to the back of the flower.

Fuse circle to back of flower.

Optional: Satin stitch around the edge of the sunflower center on the front side.

5. Measure the center point of the flower and poke a small hole with the point of a scissor blade though all the layers to insert the stem wire.

6. Insert floral stem wire up through the hole in the underside of the flower and up through one hole in the button.

7. Bend the top 1½″ of wire completely over and insert it back down through the second hole in the button and through the flower to the underside.

Bring stem wire up through flower and button and back down to underside.

fast!

If the covered wire is too thick to go through the hole in the button, remove a couple of inches of covering to expose the plain wire.

fun!

Use decorative stitches on your sewing machine to stitch embellishments on the flower center.

8. Twist the short end of the wire around the long end to secure the button and flower on the wire.

9. Wrap enough floral stem tape around the stem wire at the base of the flower to hold the flower in place.

Optional: If you want to add leaves, make them following the directions on pages 53–57.

10. Continue wrapping floral stem tape down the stem wire.

Wrap several layers of tape around stem under flower to hold flower in place.

easy!

Make a no-sew kids' version out of felt. Cut one center circle, one fast2fuse circle (both 4″ in diameter), and a petal circle (6″ in diameter). Fuse the center circle to one side of the fast2fuse and fuse the other side of the fast2fuse to the petal circle. Clip the petal circle, add the button and stem, and it's done!

fast!

Don't want to stitch around the center? Add spots of fusible web under the edges of the center, if needed, to make sure it's firmly fused. Then color around the edge of the fast2fuse with permanent marker to hide the white rim.

Have you ever seen a field of sunflowers? Get busy and make some more! Try inventing your own variations.

Shelby's Spring Flowers, Karen Flamme, 22½″ × 28½″. These flowers are just too vibrant to lie flat on a quilt!

Variations

A: Jazz up the basic sunflower with two petal layers and lots of decorative stitches in the center.

B: Wrap fluffy yarn around the wire holding the button for an unusual center.

C: Vary cuts on the edges of the center and petal circles and assemble without fusing the center to the petals.

D: Make 2 centers and vary the petal cuts for this patriotic posy.

calla lily

Calla lilies are tall, elegant white flowers that always make me think of spring. But any time of year is perfect for fabric callas that bloom in polka dots, prints, sheers, sparkles, or any fabric of your choice.

What You'll Need

Basic Supplies:

See All the Basics, pages 5–10.

Fabric:

☐ 2 squares, at least 8½″ × 8½″, of same or complementary fabrics

Fusible:

☐ 1 square, at least 8½″ × 8½″, of fusible web such as Wonder Under

Note: You'll need 2 squares of fusible web if using Timtex or canvas stabilizer.

Stabilizer:

Timtex, canvas, or fast2fuse make a stiffer, more open flower. If you want a softer flower or are using sheer fabrics, skip the stabilizer layer.

How-Tos

cutting

Use a rotary cutter, mat, and ruler to cut the following:

☐ 2 squares, 8½″ × 8½″, of flower fabrics

☐ 1 square, 8½″ × 8½″, of fusible web

Optional stabilizer:

☐ 1 square, 8½″ × 8½″, of canvas, Timtex, or fast2fuse

Notions:

☐ Wrapped 18-gauge floral stem wire

☐ Roll of green floral stem tape

☐ Glitter sticks or colored chenille sticks (from craft store) for spike in flower center

☐ Template plastic, freezer paper, or tracing paper

Look for colored glitter sticks, fuzzy wired sticks, or an invention of your own for a fun flower center.

easy!

Press all the wrinkles out of the fabric, then layer the fabric and fusible web and cut through all the layers at the same time using a rotary cutter and ruler.

fusing

Without stabilizer:

1. Iron (on a dry setting) an 8½″ square of fusible web to the wrong side of one 8½″ fabric square.

2. Peel the paper backing off the fusible.

3. Carefully place the wrong side of the other fabric square on the fused side of the first square and iron, fusing the 2 fabrics together.

With stabilizer:

fast2fuse: Iron the wrong sides of the fabric squares directly to the fast2fuse.

Canvas or Timtex: Adhere fusible web to both sides of the canvas or Timtex stabilizer, then fuse the fabric squares to both sides of the stabilizer.

fast!

Save a cutting and fusing step by using fast2fuse stabilizer.

cutting flower shapes

Please see page 60 for Calla Lily pattern.

1. Trace the flower pattern onto template plastic, freezer paper, or tracing paper, and cut it out. Feel free to enlarge or reduce the pattern if you want to make a smaller or larger flower. (You will need to start with larger squares of fabric, fusible, and stabilizer if you want to enlarge it by more than ½".)

2. Center the template on the fabric sandwich and trace the shape with chalk or erasable marker.

3. Cut out the flower using scissors or a rotary cutter.

Trace template on fabric sandwich and cut.

easy!

After cutting out the flower template, place it on the fabric and move it around so you are cutting the exact section of fabric you want.

fun!

When you use Timtex or fast2fuse, satin stitch around the flower edges with a contrasting or variegated thread to hide the white edge before you attach the flower to the stem.

assembling

1. Do any decorative stitching or fusing first.

2. Bend the top 1" of the stem wire over.

3. Select a glitter stick or fuzzy stick for the center spike. Cut to 5" in length.

4. Fold the center spike in half and attach it to the bent stem wire by twisting it on.

Bend spike and fasten to stem wire.

5. Wrap the base of the flower shape tightly around the top of the stem wire (below the center spike).

6. Hold the flower around the stem with one hand and wrap the base tightly with floral stem tape.

Fold one side of flower base over other side and hold tightly.

fast!

Add color and interest by fusing free-form pieces of fabric to the calla shape before assembling.

fun!

Use fabric paints to decorate and shade the inside of the flower.

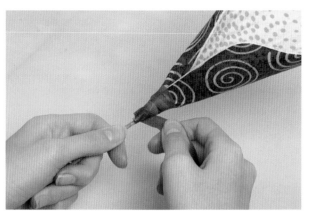

Wrap tape repeatedly around base of flower.

7. Keep wrapping tape around the base until the flower is fastened snugly to the stem, then continue twisting and wrapping the stem until it is fully covered.

Optional: If you want to add leaves, make them following the directions on pages 53–57.

easy!

Stretch the floral tape slightly as you wrap it around the stem and it will stick to itself easily. It just takes a little practice!

I'll bet you can't stop with just one! Try various fabrics and embellishments to see how different each one looks.

Variations

A: Use contrasting fabrics for the inside and the outside of the calla.

B: Fuse free-form pieces of fabric to the flower center, and satin stitch the edges with variegated thread.

C: Sheer fabrics sandwiched with fusible web make a stunning, dainty version.

D: Paint the inside with fabric paints and use fast2fuse as a stabilizer for a more open bloom.

E: Unusual textured fabric adds interest to this simple shape.

day lily

I call these day lilies, but dress them up in chic fabrics and add a few baubles and beads, and they're ready for evening. They can be big, showy blooms or small and delicate. It's up to you.

What You'll Need

Basic Supplies:

See All the Basics, pages 5–10.

Fabric:

☐ 2 rectangles, at least 9″ × 17″, of the same, contrasting, or complementary fabrics

Fusible:

☐ 1 rectangle, at least 9″ × 17″, of fast2fuse (or equivalent amount of another stabilizer and fusible web; see pages 6–7 in All the Basics). I like to use fast2fuse for day lilies, as it gives a gentle bend to the petals.

Notions:

☐ Wrapped 18-gauge floral stem wire

☐ Roll of green floral stem tape

☐ Button (or glitter sticks or yarn) for flower center

☐ Template plastic, freezer paper, or tracing paper

fun!

Get creative with the flower center. Try unusual buttons, glitter sticks, yarn, and ribbon. Use your imagination!

How-Tos

cutting

Use a rotary cutter, mat, and ruler to cut the following:

☐ 2 rectangles, 9″ × 17″, of flower fabric

☐ 1 rectangle, 9″ × 17″, of fast2fuse (or other stabilizer and fusible web)

fun!

Cut a smaller petal from another fabric and fuse it to the front of a larger petal.

easy!

If you aren't using stabilizer, fuse a piece of very thin (24-gauge) wire between fabric layers from the tip to the base of each petal to give it body and make it bendable.

fusing

1. Put a nonstick pressing sheet on the ironing board and place the fast2fuse rectangle on top. Place the wrong side of the fabric on the fast2fuse, cover with a pressing cloth, and press with a hot, dry iron until fused.

2. Turn the piece over, place the wrong side of the second rectangle of fabric on top of the fast2fuse, and iron until fused.

cutting flower shapes

Please see Day Lily Petal pattern on page 62.

1. Trace the petal pattern onto template plastic, freezer paper, or tracing paper. This makes a flower about 10˝ across. If you want a larger or smaller flower, enlarge or reduce the pattern accordingly.

2. Position the template on the fabric sandwich so that you will be able to cut 5 petals out of the rectangle. Trace the template and cut 5 petals using scissors or a rotary cutter.

Use template to mark flower petals.

If you are using fast2fuse, re-iron each petal and, while it is still warm, gently roll it backward to give a curve to the petal. It will hold this shape as it cools.

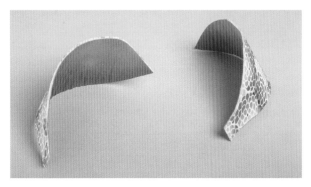

Gently roll warm petal backward.

fast!

Give the flowers a different look by rounding off the pointed ends of the petals.

assembling

Time to embellish if you want. Add decorative stitching, fused fabrics, buttons, or your own special touch.

Optional: Satin stitch around the petal edges to hide the white fast2fuse layer.

fast!

For a no-sew version, color the edge of the petal with permanent marking pen to hide the white fast2fuse layer.

fun!

Embellish petals with decorative machine stitching.

1. Select a button or embellishment for the flower center.

2. Insert floral stem wire up through the underside of the button and out one hole.

3. Bend the top 1½˝ of wire completely over and insert it down through the second hole to the underside of the button.

4. Twist the short end of the wire around the long end to secure the button on the wire.

Button attached to wire

5. Fold the base of the first petal around the stem wire just below the button.

6. Wrap floral stem tape tightly around the petal base to fasten the petal to the stem, then add the second petal opposite the first.

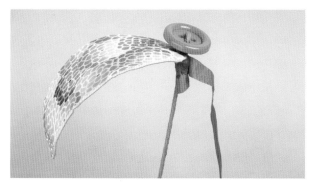

Fasten petal to stem with floral stem tape.

7. Continue to wrap tape tightly around the top of the stem, adding the other 3 petals one at a time.

Continue adding petals to top of stem.

8. Wrap the stem wire with floral stem tape, stretching it slightly as you go.

Optional: If you want to add leaves, make them following the directions on pages 53–57.

Wrap tape down stem wire.

9. To shape, bend each petal down slightly.

Now that you have mastered the technique, let your imagination go and create a day lily bouquet that will last all summer.

Variations

A: Twist glitter sticks to the center and satin stitch petal edges for a touch of glamour.

B: Fuse sheer fabric with darker accents to petals. Fuse thin wire between fabric layers from base to tip of petal to bend.

C: Textured fabrics with fused accents and fast2fuse stabilizer are perfect for a baby shower.

D: Go country with felt petals, rounded corners, edge-stitched plaid centers, and simple buttons.

E: Prints make a casual, garden-party lily.

black-eyed susan

Black-eyed Susans are easy to grow and even easier to make. You can whip up a whole bouquet without sewing a single stitch. And who says their "eyes" have to be black? Choose your favorite fabrics and fun buttons for eyes, and follow these few simple steps.

What You'll Need

Basic Supplies:

See All the Basics, pages 5–10

Fabric:

☐ 2 squares, at least 6″ × 6″, of same or contrasting fabric for front and back of flower

Fusible:

☐ 1 square, at least 6″ × 6″, of fast2fuse for fairly stiff petals

For floppier petals, use a stabilizer layer such as canvas and fusible web (or just heavyweight fusible web) between fabric layers instead of fast2fuse.

Notions:

☐ 1 button with at least 2 holes (or a shank) for flower center

☐ Wrapped 18-gauge floral stem wire

☐ Roll of green floral stem tape

easy!

Make a variety of sizes of flowers for your bouquet by reducing and enlarging the pattern on a copy machine.

How-Tos

cutting

Use a rotary cutter, mat, and ruler to cut the following:

☐ 2 squares, 6″ × 6″, of flower fabric

☐ 1 square, 6″ × 6″, of fast2fuse (or other stabilizer and fusible web)

fusing

1. Place a nonstick pressing sheet on the ironing board; fuse the wrong side of one 6″ × 6″ fabric square to the fast2fuse square by pressing with a hot, dry iron.

Fuse fabric to fast2fuse.

2. Turn the piece over and fuse the wrong side of the remaining 6″ fabric square to the other side of the fast2fuse.

cutting flower shapes

Please see Black-eyed Susan pattern on page 61.

1. Trace the flower pattern onto template plastic, freezer paper, or tracing paper and cut it out. Feel free to enlarge or reduce the pattern, depending on the size of flower you want to make. (You will need to start with larger squares of fabric if you want to enlarge the pattern.)

Cut out traced flower template.

2. Center the template on the fused fabric sandwich and trace around the flower shape with chalk or an erasable marker.

Mark flower shape on fabric.

3. Cut out the flower using scissors.

Cut out flower.

easy!

Re-iron the flower and gently bend the petals backward while warm. Fast2fuse will hold this shape when cool.

fun!

Fuse bits and pieces of contrasting fabrics to the petals, or add paint or glitter.

assembling

1. In the center of the flower, poke a hole all the way through using the pointed end of a scissor blade.

Poke hole in center of flower.

easy!

Find the flower center by folding gently in half one way, then in half again, and mark the folded center point with chalk.

2. Insert floral stem wire up through the underside of the flower and through one hole of the button.

3. Bend the top 1½″ of wire completely over and insert it down through the second hole in the button and through the flower to the underside of the flower.

4. Twist the short end of the wire around the long end.

Insert stem wire through flower and button.

Black-eyed Susan

5. Wrap floral stem tape repeatedly around the stem, just below the underside of the flower, to hold it securely in place.

6. Continue to wrap floral tape down the remainder of the stem.

Optional: If you want to add leaves, make them following the directions on pages 53–57.

Could that be any easier? Now that you've made a basic Black-eyed Susan, let your creativity loose!

Secure flower to stem with floral tape.

Variations

A: Add fuzzy yarn to the center and stitch around petals with variegated thread and decorative stitches.

B: Fuse bits of contrasting fabric to petal.

C: Cut one large and one small petal out of felt. No stitching or fusing required!

D: Fluffy yarn and fused strips on the petals add a touch of elegance to this Black-eyed Susan.

hydrangea

Big, fluffy hydrangea flowers are spectacular as a centerpiece. In the garden, hydrangea flower colors are determined by the acidity of the soil, but in the fabric flower world, hydrangeas are whatever color you can imagine!

What You'll Need

Basic Supplies:

See All the Basics, pages 5–10.

No sewing machine is needed.

Fabric:

☐ 2 rectangles, at least 10˝ × 12˝, of the same or complementary fabric for front and back of hydrangea petals

Note: This will make one hydrangea blossom with about 15 petals. I think using different fabrics for the front and back looks especially good on this flower.

fun!

Try varied shades of the same color on some of the petals in a blossom.

Fusible:

☐ 1 rectangle, at least 10˝ × 12˝, of fusible web

Notions:

☐ Unwrapped 22-gauge floral stem wire

☐ Roll of green floral stem tape

☐ Template plastic, freezer paper, or tracing paper

How-Tos

cutting

Use a rotary cutter, mat, and ruler to cut the following:

☐ 2 rectangles, 10˝ × 12˝, of flower fabrics

☐ 1 rectangle, 10˝ × 12˝, of fusible web

fusing

1. Iron (on a dry setting) the wrong side of one flower fabric rectangle to the fusible web rectangle.

2. Peel the paper backing off the fusible.

3. Carefully place the wrong side of the other fabric rectangle on the fused side of the first rectangle and iron, fusing together the fabrics for the front and back of the flower.

easy!

Keep the iron clean by placing a pressing cloth on top of fabrics to be fused before pressing.

cutting flower shapes

Please see Hydrangea Petal pattern on page 62.

1. Trace the hydrangea pattern onto template plastic, freezer paper, or tracing paper. Feel free to enlarge or reduce the pattern if you want to make a different size flower. (You will need to start with larger rectangles of fabric if you enlarge the pattern.)

fast!

The kids' version is made of felt. Skip the fusing step and cut the flower petals out of one layer of felt.

2. Cut out the template and position it on the fabric sandwich.

3. Trace the shape with chalk or an erasable marker. You should be able to cut 15 petals out of a 10˝ × 12˝ rectangle.

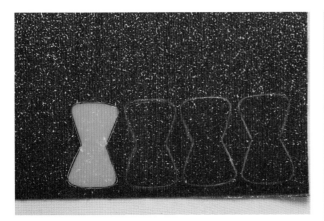
Trace around petal template onto fabric.

4. Cut out the petals using scissors.

fun!

Cut out 2 sizes of petals. Mix large and small petals in the same flower.

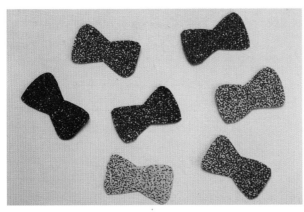
Cut out hydrangea petals.

fast!

Cut petals out of several single layers of nylon net. There's no need to fuse the layers together. Follow the assembly instructions for a fluffy, fun flower that's easy to make in party or wedding colors.

easy!

Making flowers for a festive occasion? Paint glitter on the top edges of the petals before assembling the flowers.

assembling

1. Pinch together the center of the bow tie-shaped petal.

2. Wrap the end of the 22-gauge floral stem wire around the petal center and twist tightly.

3. Leave the long end of the wire intact to use as the stem.

Wrap wire around center of petal.

4. Continue assembling all the petals.

5. Gather all the petal stems together and arrange the petals into a round hydrangea flower.

Put all petals together to make a hydrangea.

6. Gently twist the petal stems together.

7. Beginning below the flower base, wrap floral stem tape around all the stem wires to hold the flower securely together.

Optional: If you want to add leaves, make them following the directions on pages 53–57.

8. Continue wrapping the entire length of the stems.

Wasn't that easier than digging in the garden? A variety of flower sizes and colors will make your bouquet even more spectacular.

Wrap floral tape around stems.

Variations

A: Colorful nylon net makes a fluffy hydrangea, perfect for a wedding or party decoration.

B: Make a hydrangea leaf following directions on pages 54–56. Satin stitch the edges of the leaf with variegated thread and insert the flower through the hole in the leaf center.

C: Keep it simple by cutting petals out of one layer of bright-colored felt.

D: Combine two layers in each petal—one of shiny fabric, and the other of see-through net.

orchid

Orchids are so beautiful, but some people say they are temperamental and hard to grow. Not this orchid. It's the no-fuss, easygoing variety! It is no-sew, super easy, and perfect for shimmery, showy fabrics.

What You'll Need

Basic Supplies:

See All the Basics, pages 5–10.

Fabric:

☐ 2 rectangles, at least 5″ × 14″, of same or complementary fabrics for front and back of orchid flowers

Fusible:

☐ 1 rectangle, at least 5″ × 14″, of regular or heavy-weight fusible web such as Pellon Wonder Under

Notions:

☐ Unwrapped 22-gauge floral stem wire

☐ Wrapped 18-gauge floral stem wire

☐ Roll of green floral stem tape

☐ Template plastic, freezer paper, or tracing paper

How-Tos

cutting

Use a rotary cutter, mat, and ruler to cut the following:

☐ 2 rectangles, 5″ × 14″, of flower fabrics

☐ 1 rectangle, 5″ × 14″, of fusible web

easy!

Test all synthetic fabrics to make sure they won't melt when ironed. Cover the fabric with a pressing cloth and gradually heat up the iron as you gently press and check that the fabric isn't melting.

fun!

Use a shiny fabric on one side and a dull on the other for interesting contrast.

fusing

1. Iron (on a dry setting) the wrong side of one 5″ × 14″ flower fabric rectangle to the rectangle of fusible web.

2. Peel the paper backing off the fusible.

3. Carefully place the *wrong* side of the other flower fabric rectangle on the *fused* side of the first rectangle and iron, fusing the front and back flower fabrics together.

cutting flower shapes

Please see Orchid pattern on page 61.

1. Trace the orchid pattern onto template plastic, freezer paper, or tracing paper and cut out. Feel free to enlarge or reduce the pattern, depending on the size of the flower you want to make.

fast!

Use a copier to enlarge or reduce the orchid pattern. You can vary the sizes of flowers on the same stem if you want.

easy!

Fold the fabric sandwich double and cut out 2 orchid shapes at the same time.

2. Place the template on the fabric sandwich and trace the shape with chalk or an erasable marker. You should be able to trace 6 flower shapes on this size rectangle.

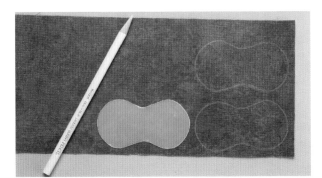

Trace around template onto fabric.

3. Cut out the orchid shapes using scissors.

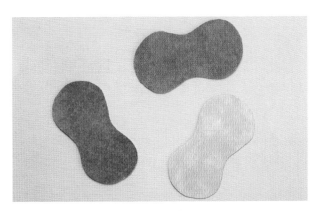

Cut out orchid flowers.

fun!

Reduce the pattern size, cut smaller orchids out of sheer fabric, and fuse them to one side of a larger flower.

assembling

Now's the time to do any decorative stitching, painting, or embellishing on the orchid flowers.

1. Cut 22-gauge wire into pieces approximately 4″ in length. You will need one piece for each orchid flower.

2. Pinch the center of the orchid flower, gathering in the sides. Fold a 4″-long piece of wire around the orchid center and twist tightly.

Pinch center of flower and wrap with thin wire.

3. Position the orchid flower where you like it on the 18-gauge covered stem wire.

4. Twist the ends of the thin wire around the stem wire to hold the blossom in place.

Fasten blossom to stem wire.

5. Continue adding as many blossoms as you want to the stem wire in the same manner.

Add blossoms.

6. Start at the top and begin wrapping the stem with green floral stem tape. Cover the thin blossom wires as you wrap the length of the stem.

Optional: If you want to add leaves, make them following the directions on pages 53–57.

Wrap stem with floral tape and bend to shape.

7. Bend the individual orchid blossoms into shape. Gently bend the stem wire.

Congratulations! You have mastered easy orchid growing. Add embellishments and try different fabrics to complete your orchid garden.

easy!

Put 2 petals together and twist thin wire around both for a different bloom.

Variations

A: Make a few larger blooms out of unusual textured fabrics and combine them with smaller plain flowers.

B: Twist two blossoms together—one of them made from sheer fabric. Decorate the stem with thin, colorful ribbons.

C: Shimmery fabrics make elegant orchids.

D: Embellish flowers with contrasting stitching before attaching them to the stem.

A   B   C   D

sweet pea

Sweet peas are often classified as early blooming or late blooming, but these bloom all year long. They are the easy, no-sew variety favored by gardeners.

What You'll Need

Basic Supplies:

See All the Basics, pages 5–10.

Fabric:

☐ 2 rectangles, at least 5″ × 12″, of same, complementary, or contrasting fabrics

Fusible:

☐ 1 rectangle, at least 5″ × 12″, of regular or heavyweight fusible web, such as Wonder Under

Note: These flowers don't need a stabilizer layer.

How-Tos

cutting

Use a rotary cutter, mat, and ruler to cut the following:

☐ 2 rectangles, 5″ × 12″, of flower fabric

☐ 1 rectangle, 5″ × 12″, of fusible web

fun!

Try sheer fabric with some shine or sparkle for fancy flowers. Just remember to test the fabric first to make sure it won't melt or pucker when ironed.

fusing

1. Iron (on a dry setting) the wrong side of one 5″ × 12″ fabric rectangle to the fusible web.

2. Peel the paper backing off the fusible.

3. Carefully place the wrong side of the other fabric rectangle on the fused side of the first piece and iron, fusing the 2 rectangles together.

Notions:

☐ Wrapped 18-gauge floral stem wire

☐ Roll of green floral stem tape

☐ Small button (or glitter sticks) for flower center

☐ Template plastic, freezer paper, or tracing

easy!

Add some zing to your sweet peas by painting on another color with fabric paints or sprinkling on some glitter.

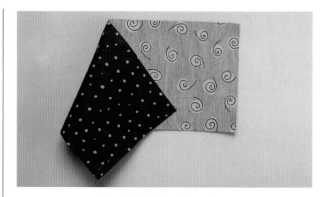

Petal fabric fused together

fast!

For the kids' version, use one layer of felt for the petals. Skip the fusing step.

cutting flower shapes

Please see Sweet Pea Petal pattern on page 62.

1. Trace the sweet pea pattern onto template plastic, freezer paper, or tracing paper and cut out.

fun!

Reduce or enlarge the petal size slightly and trace again onto template plastic, freezer paper, or tracing paper. Combine 2 sizes in one flower, using smaller petals for centers.

2. Position the template on the fabric sandwich so 5 petals can be cut from the rectangle. Trace the template and cut 5 petals using scissors.

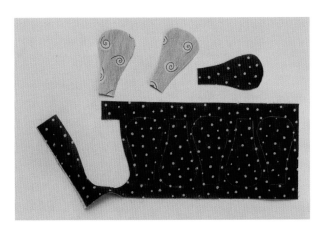

Cut 5 petals.

assembling

1. Select a *small* button for the flower center. Insert floral stem wire up through the underside of the button and out one hole.

2. Bend the top 1½˝ of wire completely over and insert it down through the second hole to the underside of the button. If you have trouble fitting the wrapped wire through the hole in the button, strip off 2˝ of paper wrapping at the top and use the bare wire.

3. Twist the short end of the wire around the long end to secure the button on the wire.

Button secured to wire

4. Fold the base of one petal around the stem wire just below the button. Wrap the petal tightly to the stem with floral tape.

5. Add another petal opposite the first and fasten it with floral tape. Continue adding the other 3 petals around the stem in the same manner, one at a time.

Attach petals to stem.

6. Wrap floral tape around the stem wire to the end, stretching it slightly as you wrap.

Optional: If you want to add leaves, make them following the directions on pages 53–57.

It's fun to make lots of sweet peas in different colors for a table centerpiece.

Variations

A: Single layers of felt with contrasting accents fused to them are the quickest petals possible.

B: Shiny fabrics make lovely little sweet peas.

C: Keep your blossom closed or bend the petals back for a more open flower.

D: Sheer fabrics and a glitter center make this sweet pea unique.

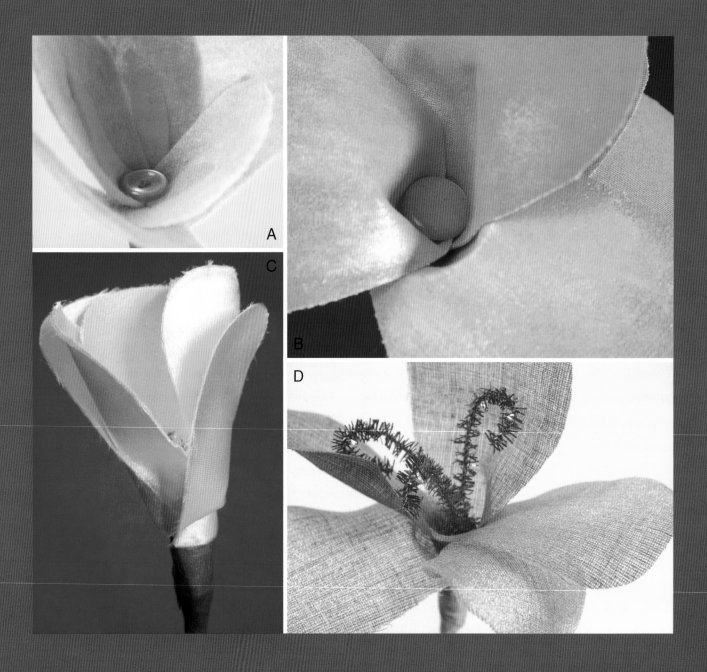

bachelor's button

Bachelor's buttons are brilliant little flashes of color. You've probably seen the familiar blue ones used as boutonnieres. Fabric bachelor's buttons make fun hair decorations, clothing accessories, and gift-wrap embellishments. These are no-sew and quick to make. Plan to have lots on hand for decorations and fashion accessories.

What You'll Need

Fabric:

☐ Pull out your scraps. These flowers take very little fabric. I like to use at least 2 different fabrics: one for the outer petals and another for the inner.

Fusible:

☐ Either regular or heavyweight fusible web

Note: These tiny flowers do not need a stabilizer.

easy!

Cut a 2½"-diameter circle of net or sheer fabric that doesn't fray. Use it as a third petal layer underneath the outer petals.

Notions:

☐ 1 small button or bead for flower center

☐ Thin, unwrapped floral stem wire, 22- or 24-gauge

☐ Needle and thread

Optional: Plain metal hairclip, jewelry pin back, or plastic headband

fun!

Use several small beads, or one large bead, in place of a button for the flower center.

How-Tos

cutting

Use a rotary cutter, mat, and ruler to cut the following:

☐ 2 squares, 3″ × 3″, from flower fabric for outer petals

☐ 2 squares, 2½″ × 2½″, from flower fabric for inner petals

☐ 1 square, 3″ × 3″, of fusible web

☐ 1 square, 2½″ × 2½″, of fusible web

fusing

1. Iron (on a dry setting) the wrong side of one 3″ fabric square to the 3″ square of fusible web.

2. Peel the paper backing off the fusible.

3. Carefully place the wrong side of the other 3″ square of fabric on the fused side of the first square and iron, fusing the 2 squares together.

4. Repeat Steps 1 to 3 for the 2½″ squares of fabric and fusible.

cutting flower shapes

Outer Petals:

1. Draw a 2½″-diameter circle on the 3″ square of fused fabric. Use scissors to cut out the circle.

2. Make ½″-deep wedge-shaped cuts from the outer rim toward the center, all around the circle, to create petals.

Cut circle; then cut narrow wedges from circle to make petals.

Inner Petals:

Draw a 2″-diameter circle with chalk on the 2½″ square of fused fabric. Use the circle as a guide to cut free-form rounded petals for the inner petals.

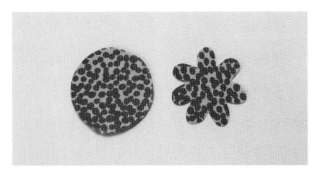

Cut rounded petals.

assembling

1. Poke a small hole in the center of the circles with the point of a scissor blade.

2. Layer the inner petals on top of the outer petals.

3. Insert floral stem wire up through the underside of the petals and through the hole in the button.

4. Turn over the top end of the wire and insert it down through the second hole of the button and the flower petals to the underside.

5. Twist the wire tightly to fasten the petals and button securely.

fast!

Instead of wire, use a needle and thread (doubled and knotted). Bring the needle up through both petal layers and the button, then back down to the underside and secure with stitches. Stitch the flower onto a little girl's shirt, hat, or other accessory.

Insert wire through petals and button.

Twist wire to hold flower together.

6. Twist the ends of the wire around a hairclip, pin base, headband, or gift-wrap ribbon to hold the flower in place. You can also use a needle and thread instead of wire.

Try a variety of fabrics and unusual centers and you'll find lots of new ways to use your crop of bachelor's buttons.

Variations

A: Twist glitter sticks around the stem wire in place of a button, and round off petal edges.

B: String a few sparkling beads onto the center wire for a classy flower.

C: Add a touch of lace to the center of a dainty baby flower.

D: Just keep adding layers—some with rounded edges, and some with straight edges.

E: *Tea Time*, Karen Flamme, 39¼″ x 28½″. Three-dimensional flowers sprout right out of these ladies' hats!

leaves

Leaves are beautiful by themselves or as backdrops to set off your colorful flowers. I'm writing this chapter in the fall, and every day the leaves turn more vibrant colors. It's a good reminder that all leaves don't have to be green. Here are instructions and patterns for making four simple leaves.

What You'll Need

Basic Supplies:

See All the Basics, pages 5–10.

Fabric:

Cottons, sheers, and felt are all good fabrics for leaves. Look for variations in color and pattern to achieve variety in texture and dimension. You can also use "leafy" print fabrics or add decorative stitching to solids to make realistic leaves. Each leaf requires just a small amount of fabric, so scraps are fine too. It's your choice whether to use the same fabric on both the front and the back of a leaf.

Coordinate the size and color of your leaf with the flower. Be sure your leaf "fits" the flower size: a big flower needs a big leaf. Audition leaf fabric colors and textures next to the flower.

Fusible:

Fast2fuse, Timtex, or fusible web (such as Wonder Under), depending on whether you want a stiff, thick leaf, or a sheer or floppy one.

Notions:

☐ 22-gauge unwrapped floral stem wire to make a sheer leaf easy to bend and hold its shape

☐ Roll of green floral stem tape

☐ Template plastic, freezer paper, or tracing paper

fun!

Add color variation to a leaf by fusing a second color fabric to the face of the leaf.

fast!

Vary leaf sizes by reducing or enlarging the pattern on a copy machine.

How-Tos

making leaf templates

Please see leaf patterns on pages 61–62.

Choose the leaf you want to make. Here are a few suggestions for combinations that I like:

Lily Leaf and Sunflower Leaf: Use in various sizes with day lilies, calla lilies, orchids, sunflowers, black-eyed Susans, and sweet peas.

Hydrangea Leaf: Use with hydrangeas and both single and double daisies.

Maple Leaf: Use several together on a stem or combine with a flower of your choosing.

Trace the leaf pattern onto template plastic, freezer paper, or tracing paper. Cut out the leaf template.

Cut out leaf template.

easy!

Have fall foliage any time of year. Make maple leaves from vibrant red, orange, and golden-yellow fabrics.

cutting

Use scissors or a rotary cutter, mat, and template to cut the following:

☐   2 pieces of leaf fabric slightly larger than finished leaf

☐   1 piece of fusible slightly larger than finished leaf

fusing

For a stiff, thick leaf: Use fast2fuse or Timtex for the center layer.

For a sheer, thin leaf: Simply fuse the front and back leaf fabrics together with fusible web.

Make a fabric sandwich by fusing the leaf fabric to the front and back of the center layer (fast2fuse, Timtex, or just fusible web). Be sure the wrong sides of the leaf fabric are next to the fusible before you iron.

To give extra body and flexibility to a sheer leaf, insert a piece of thin, 22-gauge wire between the front and back fabrics before you fuse them together with fusible web. This will create the center vein of the leaf when you cut out the leaf shape.

Insert thin wire before fusing.

cutting leaf shapes

1. Position the template on the fabric sandwich and trace the leaf shape with chalk or erasable marker. If you have fused in thin wire, be sure it is lined up with the center of the leaf from top to bottom.

Trace leaf shape.

2. Cut out the leaves using scissors or a small rotary cutter.

3. Add decorative stitching or embellishing if desired. Stitch leaf veins either by hand or machine, satin stitch leaf edges, or add glitter or paint.

fun!

Hand stitch a few beads on the leaf to add dewdrops and shimmer.

fast!

Want to hide the white edge of fast2fuse or Timtex without sewing? Paint the edge with marker or fabric paint.

assembling

1. Fold the bottom of the leaf around the wrapped flower stem.

2. Hold the leaf tightly to the stem and wrap it with floral stem tape until it is fastened in place.

3. Position additional leaves along the stem if desired and fasten as above.

4. Gently bend the leaf to a pleasing shape.

Fasten leaf to stem with floral tape.

easy!

Shape a fast2fuse leaf before fastening it to the stem by pressing it again with a hot iron and bending it into shape while still warm.

You are on your way to creating a forest! Look for more interesting leaf shapes to make, and have fun with embellishments.

Variations

A: Patterned, leafy fabrics make beautiful leaves.

B: Fuse contrasting fabric to the center of your leaf.

C: Sheer fabrics are also fun for fused accents.

D: Try colorful prints. Remember, all leaves aren't green!

E & F: Decorative stitching makes leaves look more realistic.

ideas & inspiration

A: Add sparkle or sophistication to your favorite outfit with a fabric flower pin. Fasten a purchased pin back to your blossom in place of a stem.

B: Who wouldn't smile into a mirror with this happy sunflower glued onto it?

C: A special gift is topped with a fabric flower.

D: Decorate a basket with flowers to match your party color scheme or brighten up a room.

E: Choose fabrics that match a favorite dress, then make orchid or hydrangea blossoms and wire them to a purchased headband or comb.

F: Embellish plain hairclips with your fabric flowers.

G: Whether your table setting is casual or elegant, it will be stunning with flower napkin rings. They can easily serve as placeholders too!

H: Have fun finding glittery fabrics and making them into a sparkly bouquet for a special occasion.

I: Bachelor's buttons stitched onto purchased baby shirts turn them into designer togs. Pair them with a decorated candle for a perfect baby shower gift. Be sure to stitch buttons on securely.

J: Let your imagination go! Learn to make the flower shapes in this book, then create your own.

Patterns

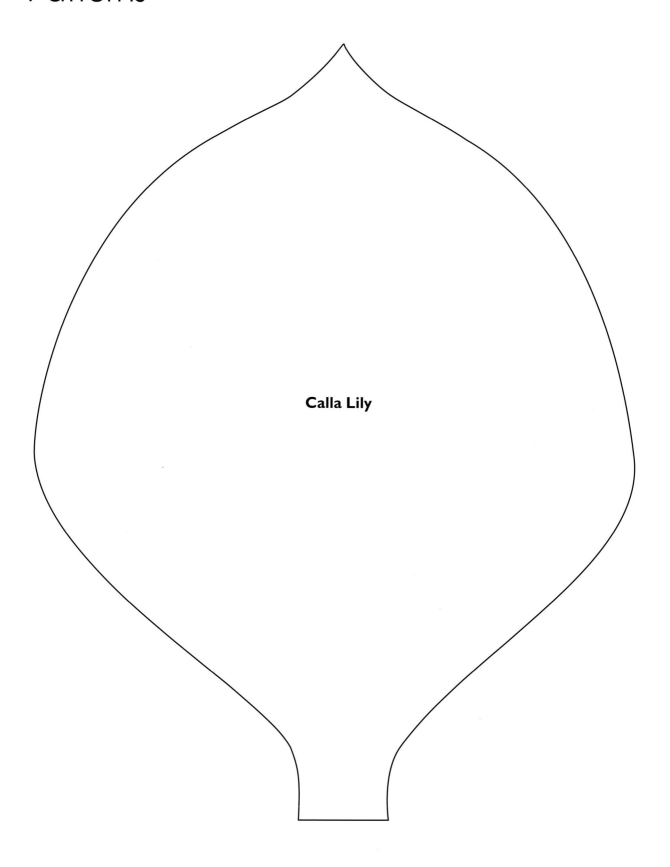

Calla Lily

fast, fun & easy FABRIC FLOWERS

Black-eyed Susan

Lily Leaf

Maple Leaf

Orchid

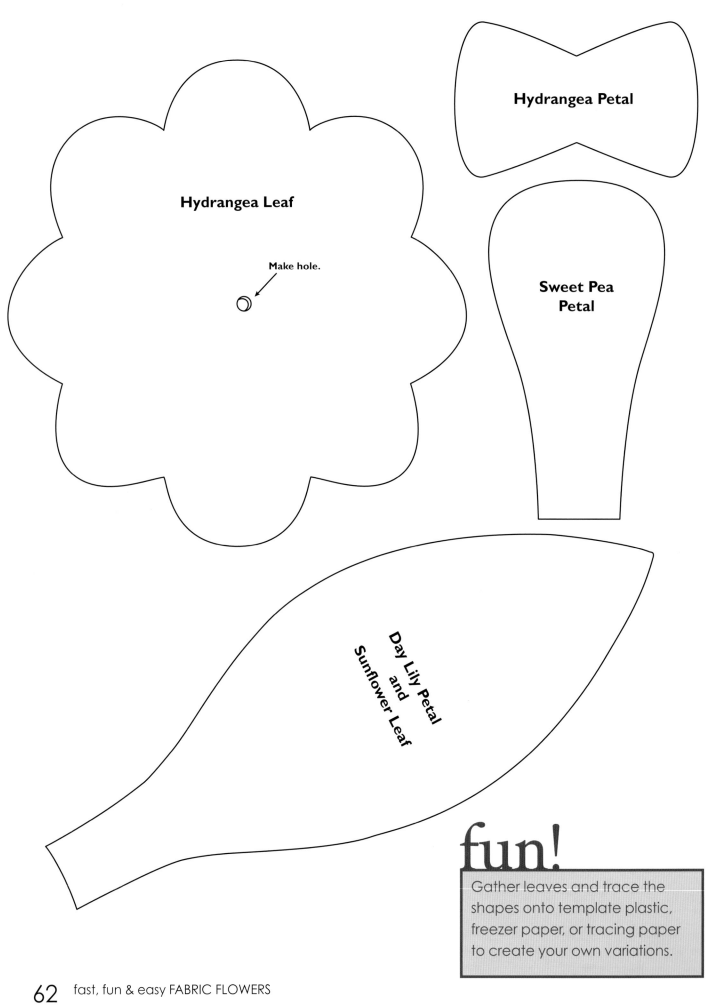

Hydrangea Petal

Hydrangea Leaf

Make hole.

Sweet Pea Petal

Day Lily Petal and Sunflower Leaf

fun!

Gather leaves and trace the shapes onto template plastic, freezer paper, or tracing paper to create your own variations.

About the Author

Photo by Jennifer Thomas

Karen Flamme is enjoying a second career as a fiber artist and writer, combining two of her favorite creative passions. In an earlier career she wrote and produced award-winning corporate communications, but even then, sewing and making art were a big part of her life. She began by sewing clothes for herself and her daughter, then embellished garments for others under her Thread Bear label.

Quilting is a natural extension of her love for color, texture, and design. Karen began making art quilts more than a decade ago. Her work is now exhibited widely in juried shows and hangs in numerous private collections. She teaches workshops in art quilting and always loves to learn from her students!

Making art and writing about it fill Karen's time when she is not finding inspiration from the garden, the beach, or fabulous friends and family. Karen is co-author of *Thinking Outside the Block*, also published by C&T Publishing. She lives in Oakland and Pebble Beach, California.

Sources

For materials and tools mentioned in this book, visit your local craft store or quilt shop.

fast2fuse Double-sided Fusible Stiff Interfacing

C&T Publishing
(800) 284-1114
Website: www.ctpub.com

Timtex

Timber Lane Press
(208) 765-3353
Email: qltblox@earthlink.net

(Timtex is made exclusively for this company; they will take wholesale orders or recommend retail outlets.)

Pellon Wonder Under Transfer Web

Freundenberg-Pellon
(800) 331-6509
www.shoppellon.com

For quilting supplies:

Cotton Patch Mail Order
3405 Hall Lane, Dept. CTB
Lafayette, CA 94549
(800) 835-4418
(925) 283-7883
Email: quiltusa@yahoo.com
Website: www.quiltusa.com

For more information, ask for a free catalog:

C&T Publishing
P.O. Box 1456
Lafayette, CA 94549
(800) 284-1114
Email: ctinfo@ctpub.com
Website: www.ctpub.com

Note: Fabrics used in the flowers shown may not be currently available as fabric manufacturers keep most fabrics in print for only a short time.

fast fun & easy SERIES   From C&T Publishing

fast fun & easy CHRISTMAS STOCKINGS
Susan S. Terry

Festive Fabric Projects to Stir Your Imagination

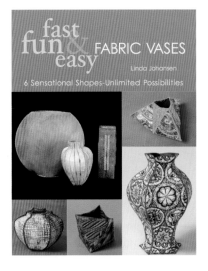

fast fun & easy FABRIC VASES
Linda Johansen

6 Sensational Shapes-Unlimited Possibilities

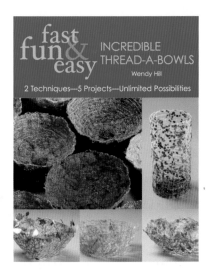

fast fun & easy INCREDIBLE THREAD-A-BOWLS
Wendy Hill

2 Techniques---5 Projects---Unlimited Possibilities

fast fun & easy FABRIC BAGS
Pam Archer

10 Projects to Suit Your Style

fast fun & easy FABRIC KNITTING
Cyndy Lyle Rymer

Fabulous Projects—Great New Looks

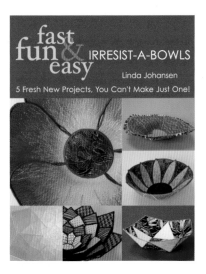

fast fun & easy IRRESIST-A-BOWLS
Linda Johansen

5 Fresh New Projects, You Can't Make Just One!

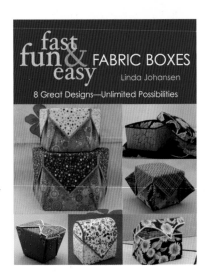

fast fun & easy FABRIC BOXES
Linda Johansen

8 Great Designs—Unlimited Possibilities

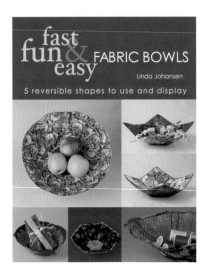

fast fun & easy FABRIC BOWLS
Linda Johansen

5 reversible shapes to use and display

fast fun & easy SCRAPBOOK quilts
Create a Keepsake for Every Memory

Sue Astroth